THE REAL CHANGE LEADER'S HANDBOOK FOR ACTION

QUENTIN HOPE AND THE RCL TEAM

FREDERICK BECKETT, STEVEN DICHTER,
MARC FEIGEN, CHRISTOPHER GAGNON,
JON KATZENBACH, AND TIMOTHY LING

TIMES BUSINESS

RANDOM HOUSE

The Real Change Leader's Handbook for Action is designed for use by readers of the book *Real Change Leaders: How You Can Create Growth and High Performance at Your Company* (ISBN: 0-8129-2626-9) by Jon R. Katzenbach and the RCL Team: Frederick Beckett, Steven Dichter, Marc Feigen, Christopher Gagnon, Quentin Hope, and Timothy Ling.

   Real Change Leaders: How You Can Create Growth and High Performance at Your Company ($27.50) is available at your local bookstore or by calling 1-800-793-2665.

THE REAL CHANGE LEADER'S HANDBOOK FOR ACTION

C O N T E N T S

THE REAL
CHANGE
LEADER'S
HANDBOOK
FOR ACTION

INTRODUCTION

WE BELIEVE THAT LEARNING FROM REAL WORLD STORIES IS CRITICAL, WHICH EXPLAINS why the book *Real Change Leaders* is based on the experiences of RCLs. However, many of our clients and colleagues have also asked for specific ways to help accelerate their change efforts. Unfortunately, there is no magic seven-step program for developing as an RCL and leading successful change programs (despite the fact that many have been promoted). Nor are there any "cookbook" formulas for handling specific situations.

The purpose of this handbook is to help change leaders by:

1. Providing a simple, informal self-assessment guide for each of the topics covered by the first seven chapters of the *Real Change Leaders* book. The diagnostic questions for each chapter are designed to quickly and simply give you a general reading on whether you are in good shape or have a lot of work to do.

2. Offering some ideas, checklists, and frameworks for getting started in areas where change leadership help is needed.

3. Providing a few pictures you may find useful in remembering and communicating to others some of the key ideas in this book.

Besides providing a starting point for thinking through your situation, this handbook may also prove helpful as a reminder of the basics to return to when things don't go as planned (and they won't!).

You will find a common theme running through the handbook, that of the "linchpin" role RCLs play within their organization (as portrayed in the following chart). It is worth keeping in mind as you work through the issues and activities of managing change in your organization. We wish you well in your essential role.

LINCHPIN ROLE OF THE RCL

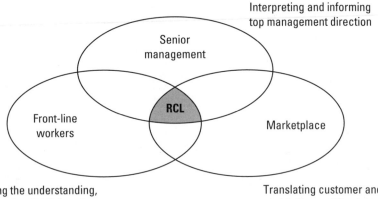

Interpreting and informing top management direction

Building the understanding, skills, and capabilities of front-line workers

Translating customer and competitor realities into operational imperatives

> **RCLs:** A new breed of managers who meld cutting edge change management skills and tools with "old-fashioned" disciplines and pragmatism

As the change leader in the middle of an organization, the RCL is in a unique position to bring together the three basic elements of effective organizational change: marketplace realities, top management direction, and workforce capabilities.

1. PERFORMANCE: DELIVERING RESULTS BEYOND THE BOTTOM LINE

A. PERFORMANCE ASSESSMENT
How clear and effective are your change objectives?

Circle your answer to the following questions:

1. Write down the performance measures you are currently expected to track and manage. How would you characterize the list?
   a) No clear measures
   b) There are more measures than anyone could keep straight; a new measure gets added every time someone gets worried about something
   c) Only one thing matters (e.g., costs, revenues, or earnings); no one really looks at anything else
   d) Most things that really matter are there; not too many, not too few

2. Using the same list of measures, mark who is served by each measure: shareholders, customers, or employees. What is the mix?
   a) No clear measures
   b) Shareholders only
   c) Shareholders and customers
   d) Shareholders, customers, and employees

3. If asked where your company stands relative to competitors, how would you reply?
   a) Dance around the question
   b) Offer observations and anecdotes on general strengths and weaknesses
   c) Give an overall assessment of who ranks No. 1 and No. 2
   d) Cite your ranking by key measure, naming those who rank higher than you in each

4. Write down your company's or unit's most aggressive current goal. How would you rate it in terms of "stretch" as well as realism?
   a) Small improvement over current performance
   b) Matches competitors' best
   c) Sets world-class standard (cross-industry)
   d) Totally unrealistic; disconnected from any sense of reality

5. Choose three employees currently working on special change projects. Ask them the objective of the project. How does each answer?
   a) With no clear answer (or no change projects under way)
   b) With an "activity-based" answer (e.g., build a customer database; train 80 people)
   c) With a clear, measurable performance goal for shareholders, customers and/or employees (e.g., cut order fulfillment time by 50% in 12 weeks)

SCORING

Score your answers as follows and then sum your total score.

		Question:				
		1.	2.	3.	4.	5. (three respondents)
Answer:	a)	0	0	0	0	0 per person _____
	b)	1	1	1	3	.5 per person _____
	c)	1	3	3	5	2 per person _____
	d)	5	5	5	0	

Your total score: _____

SCORING ASSESSMENT

You have the benefit of an organization which already has a strong performance focus. Use this base to spread and deepen change efforts.	21 to 26
You have a large role to play in building a performance focus for your organization. This is a good place to begin establishing and/or revitalizing your change effort.	5 to 20
If your organization is not already in serious trouble, it may soon be. Make sure top management is committed to the major turnaround required.	0 to 4

B. TAKING ACTION

DRAWING A PICTURE OF PERFORMANCE

If your change initiatives have a true performance focus, you should be able to describe it succinctly on a single page. Try it, using the template below (fashioned after the Sealed Air and GE Motors performance pictures from Chapter 1, pages 44 and 56).

PERFORMANCE PRIORITIES	MEASURES	GOALS
1.	a.	
	b.	
	c.	
2.	a.	
	b.	
	c.	
etc.		
If you reach more than five performance priorities, go back and question whether they are all truly priorities	Match measures to each priority, but limit yourself to no more than three per priority	For each measure, specify a quantifiable or observable goal; be sure to include "by when"

For assistance in completing this template, consider these notes and pointers.

PERFORMANCE PRIORITIES . . . WHAT REALLY MATTERS AND WHY

Performance priorities are the few things that must be done well for an organization to succeed. Think of them as actions that must be taken or conditions that must be achieved. They vary for every enterprise depending on its market and strategy, for example:

ENTERPRISE	PRIORITY	WHY IMPORTANT
Long-distance carrier	Customer retention	High cost of acquiring a customer
Hotel	Occupancy rate (utilization)	High fixed costs
Metal fabricator	Scrap rate	High raw materials costs
Computer sales force	Knowledge of customer's business	Ability to meet customer needs

ROCK-SOLID LINKAGES

A short list of performance priorities does not mean they are so high level and abstract that they have no meaning to the front line. Make sure your list has a grounding in real work. As a test, choose three individuals who are in front-line positions. Trace the linkages between your performance priorities and the actions they regularly take and the things they can control. It is unlikely every position will link to every priority, but every person should link to at least one. Here's how MEPUS (pages 29–39, Chapter 1) linked a very high-level priority all the way down to a production crew.

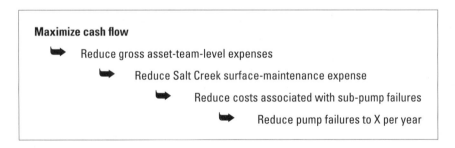

Maximize cash flow
➡   Reduce gross asset-team-level expenses
  ➡   Reduce Salt Creek surface-maintenance expense
    ➡   Reduce costs associated with sub-pump failures
      ➡   Reduce pump failures to X per year

The right, short list of performance priorities will withstand the scrutiny of several audiences:

1. For top management, it covers the necessary elements for taking the organization in the direction and to the level of performance they have targeted.

2. For employees, it is tangible, sensible, actionable, and meaningful. Imagine it as the handful of things that you would tell a new employee are the essential things to understand and always remember, the keys to "seeing the big picture" and finding personal meaning in working for the organization.

3. For a stock analyst, it demonstrates a keen understanding of the market dynamics and economics of your business. The analyst can write the story connecting these priorities to superior shareholder returns over time.

MEASURES

Measures can be a quagmire. Remember that they exist to help make decisions and guide action, not as an end in themselves. Here are some common measurement problems and solutions.

PROBLEM	POSSIBLE SOLUTION	NOTES AND CAVEATS
Too many	■ Prioritize	Force yourself to answer, if I could choose only one, if I could choose only two, etc.
	■ Look for leaders	A group of measures may be so interrelated that one can stand for all
	■ Form a second string	Assign some measures for use only when problems are anticipated or indicated by main measures
Can't be measured directly	■ Find a surrogate/substitute	e.g.: customer visits per employee for measuring employee involvement
Too much effort to measure	■ Reduce frequency	If conditions don't change rapidly
	■ Reduce accuracy	If directionally correct is good enough
Too slow	■ Move upstream to the source	Redesign your information flows so there are fewer steps and delays in getting information
	■ Do your own sampling	Rather than wait for official reports, set up a network of sources who can get on a conference call and provide an early view

GOALS

Setting goals is as much art as science. In the end, they "feel right" as a balance between an easily attainable grab and an unrealistic reach, given the capabilities of the organization and the realities of the market. Test your goals against these questions:

1. Do you already know exactly what you can do to get there? If so, there is no stretch effort in getting to the goal.

2. Where will it take you in benchmark rankings? Is the advance big enough to further encourage and energize employees and impress customers?

3. Does it cross a customer satisfaction threshold? There are often significant "breakpoints" in customer satisfaction. If your goal is below such a threshold, a seemingly big improvement will make little difference to customers.

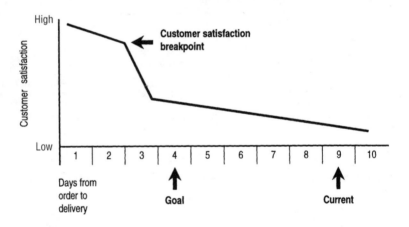

4. Will it make a significant financial difference? Reengineering a process to reduce expenses by 60% may look great, but if the process is a minor part of your cost structure, your energy may better be spent saving 15% on another process.

MAKING THE LINCHPIN CONNECTION

Merely drawing a clear picture of performance is not enough. As an RCL, you play a central, ongoing role in developing your organization's performance focus. At all times you should be making connections on three fronts.

CONNECTING MARKETPLACE REALITIES	WITH TOP MANAGEMENT ASPIRATIONS	AND WORKFORCE ENERGY AND INITIATIVE
▪ Get as many people as possible in front of customers as often as possible	▪ Stay well connected with shifts in strategy	▪ Widely share information about the business and how it is doing; create an "open books" environment
▪ Benchmark against competitors as well as "best in class"	▪ Speed and sharpen strategy planning and deliberations by bringing top management into direct contact with customer and competitor realities	▪ Clearly articulate performance priorities; translate them into terms that talk to people's daily decisions and actions
▪ Set up an ongoing "quick market intelligence" process in the style of GE Motors	▪ Provide a realistic, ongoing assessment of the organization's capabilities (how much, how fast)	▪ Explain the meaning and significance of key financial concepts (e.g., Return on Assets)
		▪ Create the pathways by which people can become engaged in meeting market challenges (see Chapter 4)

C. A PICTURE TO REMEMBER

BALANCING PERFORMANCE ACROSS STAKEHOLDERS

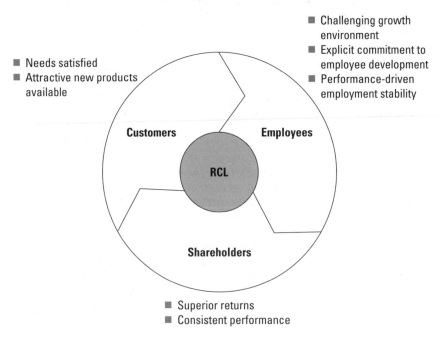

- Challenging growth environment
- Explicit commitment to employee development
- Performance-driven employment stability

- Needs satisfied
- Attractive new products available

- Superior returns
- Consistent performance

RCLs seek a self-reinforcing balance of performance objectives. Satisfying the needs of *customers* generates returns for *shareholders*, who provide opportunities for the *employees*, who deliver the value to *customers*.

2. WORKING VISION: YOU FIND IT IN THEIR HEARTS AND MINDS

A. WORKING VISION ASSESSMENT
Does a clear and compelling expression exist of what you are trying to achieve?

This assessment deals with "working visions" as opposed to overall corporate visions. Answer these questions for whatever piece of your organization's change effort is most affected by your leadership (e.g., a single project team, a number of initiatives within a certain division, or a major corporate-wide program).

Circle your answer to the following questions:

1. In single sentence or phrase, write out your working vision.

   _____

   _____

   How easy was it to write?
   a) Came immediately to mind
   b) Had to think about it a bit
   c) Had to make it up just now
   d) Drew a blank

2. Ask *three* people who are directly involved with the effort to tell you the vision.
   (i) How immediate were the responses?
      a) Right on the tip of the tongue
      b) Had to think about it a bit
      c) Drew blanks
   (ii) How consistent were the responses?
      a) Words varied some, but the same clear message
      b) Some inconsistency, but directionally similar
      c) Different for everyone
      d) No responses

3. How often can you remember the vision coming up in casual conversation, issue discussion, or decision making in the last week? Number of instances: _____

4. What are the primary personal motivations the vision draws on? Check those listed below that apply. Add others of your own.

____ Fear	____ Doing the right thing
____ Competitive spirit	____ Personal gain
____ Desire for greatness	____ Making a difference
____ _____	____ _____

How well do the motivations you checked and listed match the marketplace realities and culture of your organization? (e.g., "personal gain" is a poor fit when there is little range in pay for performance; "desire for greatness" fits well if you have inspirational leadership at the top)

a) Resonate very well
b) Could be better
c) Clear disconnects
d) No working vision

5. How would your CEO react to hearing your working vision?

a) Already heard it; great job making corporate vision relevant
b) Hadn't heard it; sounds good
c) Hadn't heard it; now very worried
d) No working vision to tell him or her

SCORING

Score your answers as follows and then sum your total score.

		Question:					
		1.	2. (i)	2. (ii)	3.	4.	5.
Answer:	a)	5	5	5	Give one point for	5	5
	b)	3	3	3	each instance	3	3
	c)	1	0	1		0	0
	d)	0		0		0	0

Your total score: _____

SCORING ASSESSMENT:

You've got it; keep it spreading; watch for the need to rejuvenate.   20+

Pieces are there, but you probably aren't realizing the practical value of a working vision; start thinking about what's needed to pull it together.

5 to 19

You are missing out on the value of a working vision; it is time to start thinking about how to initiate the process (remember, the power is in the process).

0 to 4

B. TAKING ACTION

If your working vision is lacking, here are the major pieces of the process to think through and act on to develop such a vision.

TIMING

Think of a time within the last month when it might have been opportune to introduce a discussion on "What are we really trying to do here anyway?" (e.g., a meeting where discussion was going on and on with no particular enthusiasm or action). Now think of an upcoming situation where you could be prepared to initiate the dialogue.

- Will the right mix of people be there?

- Will the group have the right context and facts for an informed dialogue?

- How would you initiate the conversation? (Something other than "Let's talk about our vision.")

PARTICIPATION

For the piece of the change effort you are leading, think about who should be involved in the process of developing a working vision.

- Who are the right individuals to involve?

- Have you included a diverse set of perspectives? Are there skeptics in the lot?

- Should they all be involved from the start? Would starting with a smaller group be more effective?

- If you decide to start small, how will you expand the participation?

- Should someone other than yourself initiate or lead parts of the discussion? How will you make that happen?

FACTS AND CONTEXT

Are there major internal actions or critical decisions planned that any vision discussion should be part of or bear in mind? e.g.:

___ Merger or acquisition   ___ Strategy review   ___ Major headcount reductions
___ New product launch   ___ Leadership change   ___ Formal reorganizations

What facts about marketplace realities (customers and competitors), performance priorities (shareholder interests), and the workforce should be known and kept in mind in any vision discussion? e.g.:

MARKETPLACE REALITIES	SHAREHOLDERS	EMPLOYEES
___ Existing strategy	___ Financial expectations (e.g., earnings growth, cash flow, ROA)	___ Satisfaction surveys
___ Target markets		___ Available incentives
___ Market share	___ Investment hurdle rates	___ Demographics
___ Customer satisfaction surveys	___ Ownership shifts	___ Turnover trends
___ Competitors' strengths and weaknesses		___ Skill gaps
___ Competitive benchmarks		___ Compensation distribution

Is this information widely enough known for there to be an informed dialogue? Do you need a period of exposure to and discussion of these facts before getting to a vision?

FACILITATING THE DIALOGUE

To get the dialogue flowing, be prepared with some tools for stimulating and capturing discussion:

■ Stories of other working visions (from the *Real Change Leaders* book or, better yet, from elsewhere in your organization or your industry, i.e., the competition!)

■ Brainstorming techniques (they are applicable here; remember Val Micklus' team's use of Post-Its to get the ideas up on the board where everyone could see them, as described on pages 82–84 of Chapter 2)

C. A PICTURE TO REMEMBER

HOW WORKING VISIONS WORK
Example: A team reengineering human resources processes for a long distance telephone service sales force

Right timing and context	Right people	Grounding in facts	Understanding of motivations
■ Frustration with just going through the motions ■ Pressing need to pull work together	■ Whole team	■ Several weeks of rolling around in data collection, interviews and analysis completed	■ Pride in company ■ Desire to serve customers well ■ Determination to make life better for salespeople in the field

INTENSE DIALOGUE

A few words that matter

"Be our customer's best sales relationship"

Relevant	Memorable	Motivating

■ Clarified real purpose of reengineering: serving customers
■ Focused redesign on critical questions
  – What makes the best relationship?
  – What experience/skills needed?
  – Who to hire
  – How to develop skills
	■ Just a few words
	■ Focused on *customers* and *relationships*, the basis of sales excellence
		■ Set high aspiration: not just the best long distance service sales relationship, but the best of *any* sales relationship
		■ Got team reoriented from HQ "staffy" work back to field perspective

A period of intense dialogue is at the heart of the process of developing a working vision. The RCL plays an essential role in assuring the right factors come into place for that dialogue to occur and assessing whether the working vision is really working.

3. COURAGE: DOING THE RIGHT THING

A. COURAGE ASSESSMENT
Is there adequate courage to take the risks of change?

Check the column for how often each of the following situations occurs:

1. In regard to your own behavior, do you:

	Almost always	Usually	Occasion- ally	Rarely
a) Remain quiet in meetings when important information or issues are missed or misconstrued	___	___	___	___
b) Avoid taking new assignments unless the odds of succeeding and looking good are high and the career risk is low	___	___	___	___
c) Accept obstacles if they are a matter of existing policy, practice, or top management guidelines	___	___	___	___
d) Avoid taking a chance on "mavericks" or unproven people if there is a safer alternative	___	___	___	___
e) Find yourself repeatedly complaining about the same things and people	___	___	___	___

2. In regard to the behavior you observe in others you work with, do they:

	Almost always	Usually	Occasion- ally	Rarely
a) Drag their feet on change in hopes that management will turn over or lose interest before anything has to happen	___	___	___	___
b) Settle for any fix that gets them through a problem rather than holding out for a real solution	___	___	___	___
c) Say "it's not my problem," as an acceptable reason for inaction	___	___	___	___
d) Say "you can't do anything about that," as an acceptable explanation for inaction	___	___	___	___

	Almost always	Usually	Occasion-ally	Rarely
e) Let some things go unmeasured because they really don't want to know or want others to know current performance	___	___	___	___

3. In regard to the behavior you observe in top management, do they:

a) Have significant differences on change direction that are tacitly recognized but not directly addressed	___	___	___	___
b) Distance themselves as initiative sponsors when things don't go well	___	___	___	___
c) Make decisions which reinforce the very practices and attitudes you are trying to change	___	___	___	___
d) Pay great attention to launching major change initiatives but shift attention elsewhere once the hard work begins	___	___	___	___
e) Protect themselves in advance from any blame should initiatives go awry (e.g., by securing lots of sign-offs or couching decisions in caveats and disclaimers)	___	___	___	___

SCORING

Score your answers for all the questions as follows and then sum your total score.

	Almost always	Usually	Occasionally	Rarely
Total number of checks:				
Scoring:	0 for each check	1 for each check	2 for each check	3 for each check
Subtotal:				

Your total score: _____

SCORING ASSESSMENT:

You have a solid base of courage to work from. The work won't be any easier, but you and others will be far more likely to persevere and succeed.	38 to 45
A good deal of courage remains to be built. Begin by building your own conviction, confidence, and courage; then go about building it in others.	16 to 37
You should seriously question whether there is a sufficient base of courage for you to lead an effective change effort. Other environments may be more rewarding for you (assuming your behavior is not driving the low score).	0 to 15

B. TAKING ACTION

MAPPING COMMITMENT

Lack of commitment is rarely uniform across an organization. The chart below is a simple template for mapping the current terrain of courage within your organization. Note the labeling of the two axes. The horizontal axis includes conviction and capability as supports of courage. A weakness in either is likely to make it hard to develop courage. Therefore, it is important to assess them as well. Only when all three attributes—conviction, capability and courage—are strong, will you have strong commitment.

The vertical axis covers the three areas in which RCLs must build courage. You can begin your assessment with these groups in general (e.g., all of your fellow department heads), but it will be most valuable when you put specific names on the vertical axis and assess them as individuals. By mapping at this level, you can identify who in particular needs help and on what dimensions.

This is a difficult exercise. It is easy to quickly characterize people as "not committed" or "uncourageous." Try to understand and empathize with other people's perspectives in order to find the best ways to reach them and gain their commitment. Remember, most people are trying to do what seems right from their point of view.

	CONVICTION $\rightarrow$	**COURAGE** $\leftarrow$	**CAPABILITY**
	Firm belief that a) change is needed, and b) the change direction is right . . . an intellectual commitment	Willingness to "do the right thing" and take on the necessary personal and professional risks and sacrifices . . . a "gut," emotional commitment	The ability to act effectively on commitments . . . a matter of talent, skills, experience, and support
Yourself			
Others around and below you			
Top management			

How to complete the map:

Jot down the pluses and minuses you see for each individual, based on your general observations and knowledge. This can also be done with trusted colleagues to get a more rounded calibration. Here's a sample assessment:

	CONVICTION	→	COURAGE ←		CAPABILITY
Jim Olden (purchasing dept. head; critical to success of product design reengineering team)	− Sees no big issues in product design process (sees main problem as sales) − Doesn't see big role for purchasing in improving design process − May think entire reengineering effort is just a fad pushed by some for their own glory		+ Good record of taking on tough projects (department consolidation in '93) + Always willing to speak his mind (reamed CEO for awarding Acme contract)		+ 20 years experience + Knows vendors' capabilities intimately − Probably doesn't understand reengineering concept and mechanics

In this situation, some simple fact sharing (to build conviction) and exposure to reengineering (to build capability) would probably go a long way in building Jim's overall commitment.

BUILDING COMMITMENT

With a better understanding of where and why there are courage gaps within your organization, you can focus your efforts. Remember, though, that courage is not an easy issue to address directly. It is built in the context of developing and leading the overall change effort. Here are some suggested actions which will help build courage and make for a stronger change program.

IN YOURSELF	IN OTHERS AROUND YOU	IN TOP MANAGEMENT
▪ Commit, even when unsure	▪ Force reality into the picture —Go to the source for the facts (customers, competitors, and your own front line)	▪ Get new/better information on the table
▪ Build your conviction and credibility —Know the facts and issues	—Don't hedge or gloss the truth	▪ Disclose your own uncertainties to encourage disclosure by others

IN YOURSELF	IN OTHERS AROUND YOU	IN TOP MANAGEMENT
—Walk the talk —Give others due credit and limelight ■ Speak out when and where it matters ■ Take bold actions which break norms to clear obstacles ■ Look to the conviction and courage of others to renew your own	■ Help translate high-level aspirations and performance priorities into meaningful terms for the entire organization (see chapter 1) ■ Reach the hearts and minds of *individuals* by appealing to a clear and compelling working vision (see chapter 2) ■ Create a contagious environment —Create early wins —Celebrate and reward success —Create a trial/lab site where others can see for themselves —Use newly-won converts to spread the word —Focus on converting well regarded skeptics —Recognize, accept, and learn from setbacks and failures ■ Take risks —On people with promise —On new tools and approaches	■ Point out inconsistencies in direction ■ Provide a window on how their actions ripple through the organization (for better and worse) ■ Share successes (large and small, group and individual) to show organization's ability to change

C. A PICTURE TO REMEMBER

THE VIRTUOUS CYCLE OF INSTILLING COMMITMENT
Waste management company example

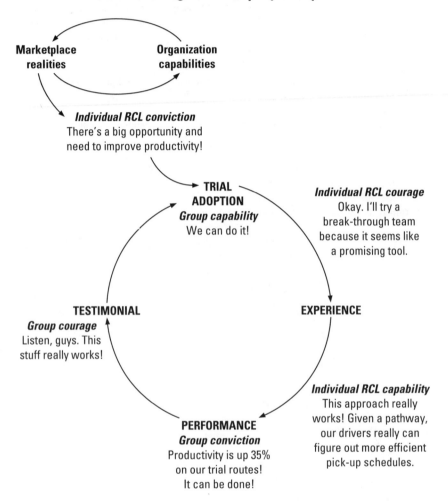

Commitment to change in an organization is built through a virtuous cycle that depends on RCLs to initiate it. Beginning with their own conviction, courage, and capability, RCLs provide the pathway for others to develop their conviction, courage, and capability. These others, in turn, infuse the wider organization with these qualities.

4. PEOPLE: GETTING EVERYONE PERFORMING ABOVE EXPECTATIONS

A. ENERGIZING ASSESSMENT
Are pivotal groups of people productively working on the highest priority goals?

Circle your answer to the following questions:

1. When the term "empowerment" is used in your organization, which phrase best describes what it means to people?
   a) No one is really sure
   b) Bosses have to listen to what employees think and let them make more decisions
   c) Employees have to work harder
   d) Employees have greater authority and responsibility to act; they are also accountable for results
   e) Employees have greater authority and responsibility to act, have the tools, training, and processes to do so, and are accountable for results

2. What results has your organization had in the past from major performance-improvement programs (e.g., quality or reengineering)?
   a) Turned out to be just another "program of the year" largely ignored by the organization
   b) Lots of effort, activity, and spending, but little real performance improvement; interest eventually faded
   c) Good short-term gains; people feel good about it, but no real change in skills and attitudes of people
   d) Real success on one dimension (e.g., cost reduction), but other critical dimensions still lag (e.g., revenue growth)
   e) Fundamentally changed the way the company operates; people more engaged and higher performing; big gains already realized and continuing on multiple dimensions

3. How clear is the pathway of your current (or recent) change initiative? Check the column which applies on these dimensions:

	Don't have/ isn't done	Poor	Good	Excellent
a) The performance goal is clear (and measurable) to all	_____	_____	_____	_____
b) People know what is off limits and what is in bounds	_____	_____	_____	_____
c) The right people with the right skills are involved; everyone is working on what matters	_____	_____	_____	_____
d) There is a clear, effective, and widely used process for solving problems	_____	_____	_____	_____
e) Work plans with tasks, responsibilities, work products, and due dates exist and are closely followed and updated as needed	_____	_____	_____	_____
f) Leadership at the top and in the middle provides direction and encouragement and clears obstacles	_____	_____	_____	_____
g) Everyone knows and is kept updated on what is happening, why, and how it fits together	_____	_____	_____	_____

SCORING

Score your answers as follows and then sum your total score.

	Question:					
	1.	2.	3. Don't have	Poor	Good	Excellent
Answer: a)	0	0	0	1	2	3
b)	1	1	points	point	points	points
c)	1	1	for	for	for	for
d)	3	3	each	each	each	each
e)	5	5	check	check	check	check
f)						
g)						

Your total score: _____

SCORING ASSESSMENT:

You are successfully creating pathways to tap the latent potential of your people; keep refining, adapting, and expanding.	23 to 31
You are likely to be losing rather than gaining energy from your mobilizing efforts; greater attention to the basics of successful performance-improvement processes can turn results around.	8 to 22
A great deal of performance potential remains locked within your people without any pathway out.	0 to 7

B. TAKING ACTION

ASSURING THAT THE BASICS OF THE PATHWAY ARE IN PLACE

In considering how to establish or get more from your performance-improvement process, the basics are the place to begin. Any pathway for involvement that you develop or adapt requires these six elements.

KEY ELEMENT	PURPOSE	BEST PRACTICE	POOR PRACTICE
1. Clear performance goals	■ Focus effort on what counts ■ Align diverse activities ■ Provide checkpoints for assessing progress and altering pace and approach ■ Define accountability	■ Clear, simple, and concise ■ Readily measurable ■ Time bound	■ Vague and open-ended ■ Difficult to measure or observe ■ Activity based
2. Well-defined playing field	■ Sanction "meddling" across functions and processes as needed to solve the problem ■ Reduce anxiety and uncertainty ■ Release energy and ideas	■ In-bound and out-of-bound areas well defined ■ Narrow enough for focus ■ Wide enough for innovation	■ Bound by function ■ Key resources withheld ■ Declaring "any and everything fair game" when not true ■ Sacred cows left protected
3. Right people in right places	■ Right complement of skills and experience available to find and implement solutions ■ Old skills used as base to build new ones	■ Conscious choice of teams, single-leader groups, and champions ■ Mix of "old salts" and promising novices	■ Same experience and skills ■ Political representation ■ Finding a home for under-performers

Key element	Purpose	Best practice	Poor practice
4. Clear involvement process —Problem solving —Work plans —End products	■ Provide a common working approach for gathering facts, generating ideas, evaluating options, and selecting solutions ■ Facilitate wide participation and accelerate action ■ Keep everyone clear on who is delivering what, by when	■ Simple ■ Well matched to task at hand ■ Adjusted as conditions change	■ Rigid adherence to elaborate multistep processes when value not clear ■ Slipping away from work plans until soon forgotten ■ No break points for closure and celebration
5. Committed leadership group	■ Bolster conviction ■ Weigh and manage risks ■ Resolve impasses ■ Clear roadblocks and provide cover ■ Relieve confusion ■ Gain and provide insights ■ Assure individual and group accountability	■ Willing to get hands dirty ■ Nonpartisan as to function or position ■ Accessible ■ Learning oriented ■ Recognize and reward success ■ Recognize and accept failure (for right reasons)	■ Present only at kickoff, crisis, and conclusion ■ Generate make-work ■ Administration/process oriented ■ Let accountability slide ■ Deny recognition/ reward for success ■ Damn failure to achieve stretch objectives
6. Thorough communications	■ Address personal uncertainties and concerns ■ Keep big picture clear ■ Satisfy people's need to know what's going on ■ Circumvent rumor-mill distortions	■ Current and frequent ■ Matches message to audience ■ Multimedia and multilevel to reach all ■ Tells lessons learned as well as successes	■ Broad and generic; no details or facts ■ Scattered; no consistent themes ■ Posthumous ■ Good news only

Starting Small

Organizations sometimes fail to create effective pathways by trying too much too soon. Starting with a smaller scale (a single work area or location) and narrower scope (a tightly defined problem) can offer several advantages.

1. A sense of confidence in using structured processes. Many organizations are used to *unstructured* processes for improving performance (i.e., crisis management). Consequently, they may be skeptical of making the initial investment in time and thought needed to develop a structured approach. Experiencing the benefits of more performance and less turmoil that come from structured processes will convince the doubters.

2. A compressed time frame. Rather than slogging through a year-long effort before seeing if and how the process works, it is possible to cycle through from start to success in a matter of weeks. This allows a chance to review, reflect and integrate learning before starting the next iteration.

3. A chance to develop necessary group skills. Common to all flavors of performance-improvement processes is the need for basic analytic and process skills. While general management emphasizes individual skills, change management requires group skills. Starting with smaller problems allows an easier and safer (but still real) environment for groups to consciously practice these skills:

ANALYTIC SKILLS	PROCESS SKILLS	DECISION SKILLS
■ Breaking down problems	■ Group facilitation	■ Framing alternatives
■ Generating and testing hypothesis	■ Brainstorming	■ Evaluating trade-offs
	■ Meeting management	■ Assessing risks
■ Gathering and synthesizing data	■ Project management	■ Resolving conflicts

LEVERAGING WHAT IS ALREADY IN PLACE

You rarely have to start from scratch. Here are some ideas for finding pieces of experience and knowledge within your organization that you can build from:

1. Make a list of past projects that are widely viewed as having had more success than the norm. Ask the leaders and participants why they worked and what they would have done to make them better.

2. Think through any major improvement programs (e.g., a company-wide quality push), even if they largely failed. See if there are any parts of them that did stick, which could be built into a new effort (e.g., many quality programs contain excellent, step-by-step, problem-solving processes).

3. Check existing management training programs and materials for pieces that may be useful. Most organizations have accumulated a great deal of decent material on their shelves. It probably ended up there because it was not used as part of a performance-improvement process focused on a real objective.

C. A PICTURE TO REMEMBER

EMPOWERMENT THROUGH STRUCTURED PERFORMANCE-IMPROVEMENT PROCESSES

Key Elements	Why They Work	Why They Keep Working
Clear performance goals	Pathway provided for constructive participation	Enabling – new skills and successes build confidence to take on more
Well defined playing field	Complementary skills brought together; old skills build new skills	Leveragable – same process can be replicated in multiple areas
Right people in right places	New insights and solutions stimulated by everyone having new information and tools	Memorable – no need to start from scratch next time around
Clear, flexible involvement process		
Committed leadership group	Safe environment created for probing and trialing	Adaptable – basic framework of six elements can be tuned to situation
Communications	Efforts unified by a common goal	

The success of every structured performance-improvement process, from a simple problem solving effort around one machine in a manufacturing plant, to an organization-wide reengineering effort, depends on adherence to these six basic elements.

5. PROCESS: ACTIONS THAT CONNECT TO THE CUSTOMER

A. PROCESS ASSESSMENT
How well do work processes meet customer needs?

Circle or check your answer to the following questions:

1. If you lost a major customer or had a significant drop in overall sales, how and when would *you* find out?
   a) Directly from the customer or wholesaler/retailer
   b) Directly from someone in your organization who heard it from the customer or wholesaler/retailer (e.g., a key sales contact)
   c) From someone who heard it from someone in your organization
   d) From your boss
   e) From reading the regular sales or revenue report

2. Answer only the applicable question:
   (i) If you are in sales, marketing, service or other group which naturally has contact with customers, when do *you* talk to customers about their needs, how they value your product/service, ideas they have for improvement, their assessment of competitors, and similar topics?
      a) Quite regularly, as a deliberate conversation/interview entirely apart from regular sales calls or service delivery
      b) If they raise an issue or problem, as a way of flushing out their concern
      c) Sometimes in the course of making a sales presentation, as a way to further the sale, or if it comes up when servicing the customer
      d) Very rarely; there's no time and such subjects can open a can of worms
   (ii) If you are not in a group that naturally has customer contact, what percentage of the people in your work group met directly with customers sometime in the past year to discuss the sorts of subjects mentioned above?
      a) 91%–100%   c) 11%–50%
      b) 51%–90%   d) 0%–10%

3. How would you describe your organization in terms of its functional hierarchy?
   a) Functions still exist, but mainly for convenience and to develop depth of expertise; most routine work and problem solving happens fluidly across functions through teams, working groups, and other means

    b) A functional organization, but when a major issue or opportunity arises we can put together an effective cross-functional group and work things through

    c) A highly functional organization; when cross-functional issues arise you have to work them "up and over" (up to your boss and over to your boss' counterpart); most big problems get worked through but it takes time and energy; many issues and opportunities fall through the cracks along the way

    d) An extremely functional organization; you just don't raise issues involving someone else's domain unless you are willing to take it all the way to the top

4. How well do *you* work across the functions of your organization to solve problems and improve performance? Check the answer which best matches these statements:

	True	Partly true	False
a) I have very few good working relationships with effective people in other functions that I can use to get things done informally	_____	_____	_____
b) When issues involving another function arise, my first course of action is to raise it with my boss for advice or action	_____	_____	_____
c) When working with people in other functions, I spend a lot of time on internal procedures, power games, or other stuff which does very little to help customers or improve performance	_____	_____	_____
d) When participating in a cross-functional task force or group, I see my role as representing and protecting the interests of my function, department, or organization	_____	_____	_____

5. How would you describe the results of any efforts your organization has made in process redesign, reengineering, process management, or the like?

    a) There is truly a new focus by everyone on customers; we serve them better, more quickly, and at less cost by really having changed the ways we do business

b) Costs and headcount are down; customers are getting about the same value
c) Costs and headcount are down; customers are probably getting less value
d) Nothing much has really changed, except we now have more meetings to attend, more buzzwords to talk, and some added confusion in the organization
e) No efforts; no change in value delivered to customers

SCORING

Score your answers as follows and then sum your total score.

		Question: 1.	2.* (i)	2. (ii)	3.	4. True	Partly true	False	5.
Answer:	a)	5	5	5	5	0	1	2	5
	b)	3	3	3	3	points	point	points	3
	c)	2	1	1	1	for each	for each	for each	0
	d)	1	0	0	0	check	check	check	0
	e)	0							1

*Score only one part

Your total score: _____

SCORING ASSESSMENT:

You and your organization have the capability to think and act beyond functions and to look instead to customers for direction; keep using it to deliver ever better value to customers.	22 to 28
Your view of customers is limited and your ability to work across functions only occasional; keep working across functions to improve performance, one problem and opportunity at a time, until it becomes business as usual.	6 to 21
Your functional hierarchy is greatly inhibiting your ability to deliver more value to customers, cheaper and faster.	0 to 5

B. TAKING ACTION

Thinking "process" does not necessarily require launching a massive, high profile reengineering program. At its simplest, it is just a matter of: 1) identifying with the customer; 2) looking across entire actions flows across functions; and 3) working effectively across functions to solve problems. These are steps any change leader in the middle can initiate.

IDENTIFYING WITH THE CUSTOMER

Select a customer segment served by your company with which you are very familiar (or a product/service line offered). Using the template from the example below,

a) List the elements which define superior customer value for the segment (including items you may not deliver or a competitor delivers better)

b) Rate how well you currently deliver those elements (1 = poor, 5 = best in class)

c) Where low ratings appear, list two things which could be done which would most improve performance on that aspect of customer value

EXAMPLE: LONG ISLAND SUPERMARKET
CUSTOMER SEGMENT: WEEKEND CONVENIENCE SHOPPERS
(SEE PAGES 172–173 IN CHAPTER 5)

A. ELEMENT OF CUSTOMER VALUE	**B. RATING**	**C. NEEDED IMPROVEMENT ACTIONS**
1. Quick check-out	2	■ Better checkout lane staffing to match customer load ■ Eliminate "no/wrong price" items
2. Clear aisles	1	■ Adjust stocking schedule away from customer peaks ■ Reduce size of stocking dollies and size of load on dollies
3. Shopping carts in good repair	2	■ Start maintenance program ■ Reduce damage by getting shopping carts out of parking lot (they get hit by cars)

LOOKING AT ACTION-FLOWS ACROSS FUNCTIONS

Now, put together a simple process and opportunity map:

a) Based on your existing knowledge, sketch out the basic process flow(s) which are experienced by customers and through which the elements of value listed above are delivered to them

b) Beside each process step, identify the function(s)/position(s) associated with it

c) Match the needed improvements (as listed above) to the process steps

d) Identify why you think the improvement actions are not being taken

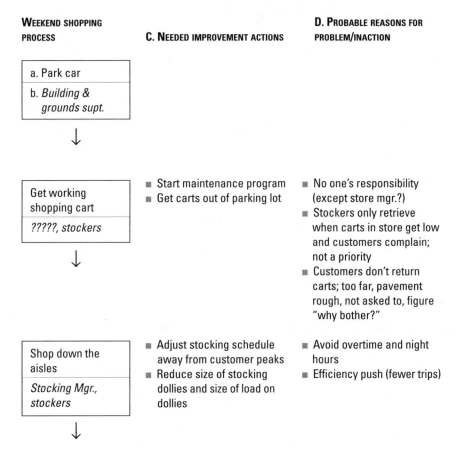

WEEKEND SHOPPING PROCESS	C. NEEDED IMPROVEMENT ACTIONS	D. PROBABLE REASONS FOR PROBLEM/INACTION
a. Park car b. *Building & grounds supt.* ↓		
Get working shopping cart *?????, stockers* ↓	■ Start maintenance program ■ Get carts out of parking lot	■ No one's responsibility (except store mgr.?) ■ Stockers only retrieve when carts in store get low and customers complain; not a priority ■ Customers don't return carts; too far, pavement rough, not asked to, figure "why bother?"
Shop down the aisles *Stocking Mgr., stockers* ↓	■ Adjust stocking schedule away from customer peaks ■ Reduce size of stocking dollies and size of load on dollies	■ Avoid overtime and night hours ■ Efficiency push (fewer trips)

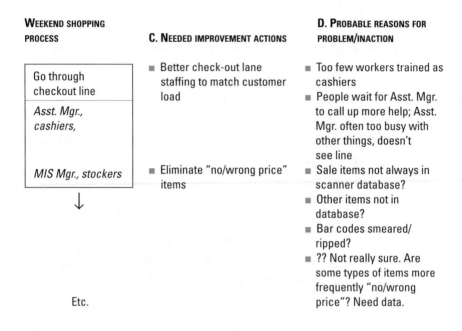

WEEKEND SHOPPING PROCESS	C. NEEDED IMPROVEMENT ACTIONS	D. PROBABLE REASONS FOR PROBLEM/INACTION
Go through checkout line	■ Better check-out lane staffing to match customer load	■ Too few workers trained as cashiers ■ People wait for Asst. Mgr. to call up more help; Asst. Mgr. often too busy with other things, doesn't see line
Asst. Mgr., cashiers,		
MIS Mgr., stockers	■ Eliminate "no/wrong price" items	■ Sale items not always in scanner database? ■ Other items not in database? ■ Bar codes smeared/ripped? ■ ?? Not really sure. Are some types of items more frequently "no/wrong price"? Need data.
↓		
Etc.		

WORK ACROSS FUNCTIONS TO SOLVE PROBLEMS

Using this quick analysis, sit down with someone from a function (other than your own) in the process flow with whom you have a good working relationship. Go through your thinking and ideas with them. Start a dialogue which can be expanded to others in other functions, with an eye toward forming a cross-functional group that can really work the issues. In holding your discussions, keep these points in mind:

1. Stay focused on customers and what matters to them

2. Don't focus only on the shortcomings of the other person's function. This is not a inter-departmental bashing session. It's a starting dialogue to solve a problem.

3. Be very open about the shortcomings in your own area

4. Revise your analysis as you talk, incorporating other's knowledge and ideas

5. Work toward identifying a problem area which you can begin working together, something that is both important and doable in the near term

Here are some typical cross-functional problem-solving actions you can look forward to achieving:

TYPICAL CROSS-FUNCTIONAL IMPROVEMENT ACTIONS

- Eliminating steps
  —Unnecessary reviews/ approvals
  —No-value-added activities
- Combining steps
  —Letting one person/group do multiple tasks

- Smoothing hand-offs
  —Eliminating errors
  —Reducing delays
  —Providing complete information

- Providing better/faster information
  —To enable front-line decision making
  —To detect errors earlier in process

C. A PICTURE TO REMEMBER

BUSINESS AND MANAGEMENT PROCESSES
Retailer example

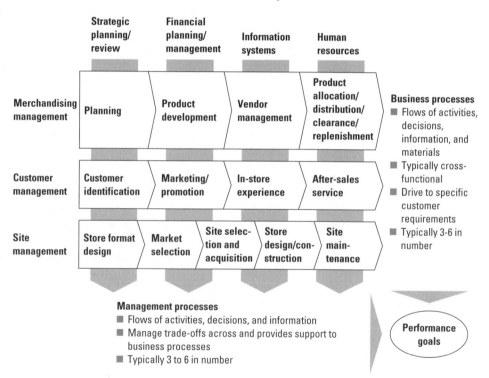

Fundamental to having a process perspective is seeing your enterprise as a collection of business processes (the action and information flows which result in major value for the customer) and management processes (the action and information flows that enable the business processes). These processes, of course, vary by industry and situation within the industry. A "generic" view of processes for merchandise retailers is shown above.

6. SPEED: ORGANIZING SKILLS FOR FLEXIBILITY

A. ORGANIZING FOR SPEED AND FLEXIBILITY ASSESSMENT
How well do formal and ad hoc structures support required changes?

RCLs seldom look to the formal organization structure as the answer to perfor-mance improvement. Instead, they use a variety of flexible approaches for align-ing and organizing people which work within and around the existing structure. Score yourself on these questions to determine how well you are using all the options available.

Circle your answer to the following questions.

1. How would you characterize the effect of the most recent change in your organization's structure?
   a) Clearly linked to performance-improvement objectives; the purpose and value was clear to all
   b) Seemed logical but no net change in performance resulted
   c) Perceived as another shuffling of the deck; definitely shifted focus inward and probably hurt performance for a time

2. Think back to the last time you faced a tough problem involving another function or department. How did you approach it?
   a) Reported the situation to my boss for resolution through normal channels
   b) Hashed it out directly with my counterparts in the other function and came up with a compromise solution acceptable to all
   c) Formed a cross-functional problem-solving group which got the facts on the table and developed new solutions leading to higher overall performance

3. Looking across your organization, how would you characterize its use of teams?
   a) No use of teams; everything managed through the formal structure
   b) Teams are launched for every new issue; everyone belongs to several; much time and attention is given to team building exercises
   c) Most teams are still single-leader working groups; more real teams are needed
   d) Teams are used in areas where new approaches and high performance are needed; other options (working groups and energized individu-als) are used elsewhere

4. Answer yes or no to the following statements about a particular team effort you are (or have recently been) part of.

	Yes	No
a) Our team is the right size: small enough to make communication easy, large enough to have the variety of people needed	___	___
b) Within the group, we have or are developing the mix of skills needed	___	___
c) We have a clear goal; achievement of our goal requires us to do real work together on identifiable collective work products	___	___
d) We share a meaningful purpose, bigger and deeper than our goal	___	___
e) We have a clear way of working together and dealing with problems	___	___
f) All team members are clear on their individual responsibilities and believe they are equally accountable for the team's overall success	___	___
g) Leadership of the team is shared and shifted as appropriate without seeking unnecessary consensus	___	___

SCORING

Score your answers as follows and then add up the total score.

		Question:				
		1.	2.	3.	4. –yes	4. –no
Answer:	a)	5	0	0	1	0
	b)	2	2	2	1	0
	c)	0	5	3	1	0
	d)			5	1	0
	e)				1	0
	f)				1	0
	g)	0			1	0

Your total score: ___

SCORING ASSESSMENT:

Very effective use of organizing options; keep varying your approach for the situation at hand.	16 to 22
Using some options but without the discipline or variety required; expand your approaches, but be very deliberate what you use where.	6 to 15
Relying too heavily on formal structure; you are limiting your performance potential by not trying other approaches.	0 to 5

B. TAKING ACTION

Managing major change presents many opportunities for making choices about how to align and organize people. If your assessment showed you were not taking full advantage of the available options, keep these points in mind.

RECONSIDER REORGANIZING

If discussion and planning for a change in your organization structure is under way, consider these questions to determine whether it is your best option.

	Yes	No
■ Is there a clear performance-improvement objective tied to the reorganization?	_____	_____
■ Would it still be necessary if personality or performance problems of particular people were not an issue?	_____	_____
■ Will the purpose of the reorganization be clear to people at the front line in terms that are meaningful to them and their work (other than potentially having a new boss or boss' boss)?	_____	_____
■ Can you articulate in a sentence the purpose of the reorganization without falling back on generalities and buzzwords? E.g.:	_____	_____

—We're forming a new group bringing together the marketing and engineering experience necessary to capture 25% of the appliance motor market within two years.

vs.

	Yes	No

—As part of our ongoing effort to respond to changing market conditions and streamline operations, we are restructuring our Southeast and Midwest divisions into a new Mid-America division.

■ Does is bring everyone closer to frontline contact with customers?

■ Does it shift functions from staff to line?

■ Does it regroup people into smaller units with a sharper focus on a distinct set of customers?

If more than two no responses appear, it is worth considering what other approaches you could take to address the issues which prompted the idea of reorganizing.

Consider Alignment and Organizing Alternatives

Changing organization structure is often seen as the fastest and easiest way to make change happen, but it is rarely the most effective. RCLs choose appropriately from a wide range of approaches for aligning organizations and getting people working on the right things. Before moving to structurally reorganize, force yourself to flush out a couple of alternatives, including:

Approach	Application
■ Clear performance objectives	■ Focus and/or accountability are lacking
■ Working vision	■ Overall sense of direction and purpose are missing
■ Performance-improvement processes	■ Problem is known, but a clear pathway showing where to start and what to do next is missing
■ Business process redesign	■ Functional focus of the organization impedes delivering value to the customer
■ Management process redesign	■ Internal practices and procedures are working against performance-improvement objectives
■ Flexible organizing units (teams, single-leader working groups, champions)	■ Particular issues/opportunities beyond the capability of the regular organization structure need to be addressed

Use Your Flexible Options Wisely

The next time you are involved in determining how best to organize people to solve a particular problem or realize a new opportunity, use this checklist to think through what might be the best flexible organizing unit to use.

	Real Team	Working Group	Champion/ Maverick
Time is of the essence, more so than extraordinary performance		■	■
Breakthrough performance is required, more than the sum of individual bests	■		
The problem/opportunity is familiar; it has been successfully worked before		■	
The problem/opportunity is new ground; the answer isn't clear; conditions and objectives may shift during the effort	■		
Activity coordination and information sharing is the main reason for bringing people together		■	
The objectives can be disaggregated and individual pieces of responsibility readily assigned		■	■
A mix of skills, working in close combination, is needed	■		
People can achieve their best working mainly alone, using the skills and knowledge they already have		■	
A strong leader is available who knows just what to do and can integrate individual work products		■	■
Many hands are needed just to get the work done		■	
Extraordinary zeal, focus and willingness to cross boundaries and break from convention is needed			■

Adhere to Team Basics

If you have chosen a real team as your organizing unit, its benefits will only be realized by vigorously adhering to six team basics. From the beginning, and periodically through the life of the team, test your team with these questions:

Team Basics	Question
1. Small enough in numbers	■ Can you convene easily and frequently? ■ Does each member understand the others' roles and skills?

TEAM BASICS	QUESTION
2. Adequate levels of complementary skills	■ Are three categories of skills represented (functional/technical, problem-solving/decision-making, and interpersonal)? ■ Are any skill areas that are critical to team performance missing or underrepresented? ■ Are the members, individually and collectively, willing to spend the time to help themselves and others learn and develop skills?
3. Truly meaningful purpose	■ Does it constitute a broader, deeper aspiration than just near-term goals? ■ Do members frequently refer to it and explore its implications? ■ Do members feel it is important, if not exciting?
4. Specific goal or goals	■ Are they team goals versus broader organizational goals or just one individual's goals (e.g., the leader's)? ■ Are they clear, simple, and measurable? If not measurable, can their achievement be determined? ■ Are they realistic as well as ambitious? Do they allow small wins along the way?
5. Clear working approach	■ Is the approach concrete, clear, and really understood and agreed to by everybody? Will it result in achievement of the objectives? ■ Will it capitalize on and enhance the skills of all members? Is it consistent with other demands on the members? ■ Does it require all members to contribute equivalent amounts of real work?
6. Sense of mutual accountability	■ Are the members individually and jointly accountable for the team's purpose, goals, approach, and work products? ■ Are the members clear on what they are individually responsible for and what they are jointly responsible for? ■ Is there a sense that "only the team can fail"?

C. A PICTURE TO REMEMBER

THE TEAM PERFORMANCE CURVE

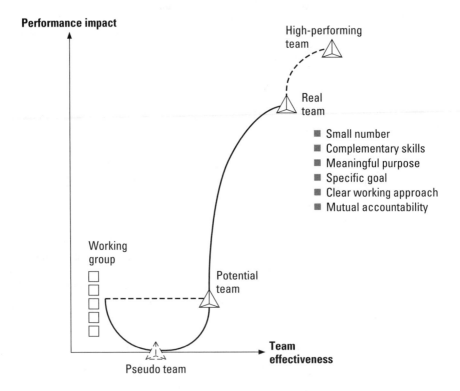

Not every group that calls itself a team will outperform a single leader working group. A dysfunctional pseudoteam will actually produce far less than if the individuals worked alone (as they essentially do in a working group). A potential team which is struggling to develop the team basics may also underperform a working group for a time, though it is headed for higher performance. A real team will always outperform a working group. In rare cases, team members go beyond the conditions for a real term and become deeply committed to one another's personal growth and development. Such high-performing teams deliver extraordinary performance.

7. MOMENTUM: SUSTAINING AND BUILDING RESULTS OVER TIME

A. MOMENTUM ASSESSMENT
Are you doing the right things to speed, spread, and sustain change?

Circle your answer to the following questions:

1. Think about performance improvement in your areas of influence.
   (i) How many *areas* delivered better value to customers at lower cost this year than last?
      a) Most—and we're working on why the others didn't
      b) About half—we're working on how to keep this much going
      c) A few—but that's the exception rather than the rule
      d) None—we're just holding on or losing ground
   (ii) How many *change initiatives*[1] delivered real, measurable performance improvement?
      a) Most—a few failed because we're really stretching
      b) All—we can see real improvement
      c) A few—we have some wins, so we're learning
      d) None—we're trying, but haven't seen results
      e) None—we haven't started any initiatives

2. Make a list of the different tools[2] you are using to involve people in solving problems to improve performance. How many are on your list?
   a) A half dozen or more—what we use depends on the situation
   b) Three or four—we're learning as we go
   c) One or two—we haven't tried anything else
   d) None—we just muddle through as we go

3. What percent of the people above, below and around you in the organization whom you influence used change tools to improve performance in the last year?

---

[1] Change initiatives are organized actions involving people in solving problems for performance improvement above and beyond the course of maintaining business as usual.
[2] Tools are structured, proven, and replicable means of accomplishing some part—large or small—of your change objective.

    a) Better than 50%   c) Less than 20%

    b) 20%–50%   d) None

4. For how many potential RCLs are you creating growth opportunities?

    a) A dozen or more   c) One or two

    b) A handful   d) None

SCORING

Score your answers as follows and then sum your total score.

		Question: 1. (i)	1. (ii)	2.	3.	4.
Answer:	a)	5	5	5	5	5
	b)	3	4	2	3	3
	c)	1	3	1	1	1
	d)	0	1	0	0	0
	e)		0			

Your total score: _____

SCORING ASSESSMENT:

Your change program is reaching critical mass; it is building momentum and capacity for continuous improvement.	19 to 25
While your change efforts are producing some gains, further progress and sustainability are remaining challenges.	5 to 18
You are starting from nearly a dead stop. A good deal of energy will be required just to overcome existing inertia and resistance. Focus first on getting tangible success in a small area, which you can then build on.	0 to 4

B. TAKING ACTION

EXPANDING YOUR TOOL KIT

Think of change tools as any structured, proven, and replicable means of accomplishing part or all of your change objective. Techniques, approaches, methods, procedures and frameworks all fall under this definition. As with carpentry or car mechanics, no one tool does it all. RCLs draw from a wide variety of tools suited to the task at hand. Some are very simple and specific in their application; others are actually combinations of tools for managing large and complex challenges.

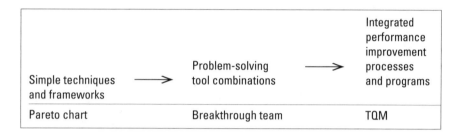

Simple techniques and frameworks	→	Problem-solving tool combinations	→	Integrated performance improvement processes and programs
Pareto chart		Breakthrough team		TQM

Under the daily press of change management it is easy to fall back on a few familiar tools and even forget some you have used before. To develop as an RCL it is necessary to consciously and proactively work to keep expanding your tool kit.

a. Think about your current change challenge and what is missing or not working. Imagine the sort of tool that would help, without worrying about what it is or if it exists. Then begin a search focused on the needs you have identified.

■ Ask other change leaders you know about tools they've used in similar situations.

■ Visit similar change initiatives at customers, vendors, related industries, and elsewhere in your company. Don't just get their official spiel, ask to sit in on some real work in progress to see how it is done.

■ Scan the change literature for ideas (books, articles, seminars, training material, etc.) Don't feel obliged to adopt whole programs; look for the pieces that may work in your situation.

b. If you aren't currently involved in any change initiative, seek out available opportunities, especially those tackling problems and using approaches with which you are not familiar.

MATCHING TOOLS TO THE TASK

Every new situation requires assessing whether you are using the right set of tools. This may be as simple as deciding if a Pareto chart is the right framework for sorting through the data in front of your team or as complex as determining if reengineering is the best performance-improvement process for increasing customer satisfaction. Here are several major factors (with illustrations) to consider in making such assessments:

FACTOR	POSSIBLE SITUATION	APPROPRIATE ACTIONS/TOOLS
Time available	Little time available	▪ Providing very clear, top-down direction ▪ Hiring/renting required skills ▪ Relying on the most change-ready/experienced people ▪ Using single-leader working groups vs. teams
Size of performance gap	Big performance gap; new solutions needed; reasonable time available	▪ Using real teams; paying close attention to team basics ▪ Broadly defining the playing field
Scale	Large numbers of people involved	▪ Assuring highly visible top leadership support ▪ Carefully planning communications ▪ Providing more formalized and packaged skills training ▪ Tightly defining the playing field (who's doing what) ▪ "Hardwiring" work plans for coordination and tracking progress
Scope	Many discrete functions involved/affected	▪ Using well designed cross-functional working groups and teams ▪ Establishing a common problem-solving approach and language
Readiness	Low on all counts: ▪ awareness ▪ conviction ▪ capability ▪ courage	▪ Building general understanding of business and performance gap for sense of urgency (a burning platform)

FACTOR	POSSIBLE SITUATION	APPROPRIATE ACTIONS/TOOLS
		■ Developing early working visions (a magnet) ■ Concentrating in one area with small groups to achieve early wins and start a "virtuous cycle" commitment building ■ Engaging opinion leaders in the organization
Data availability	Data not available or hard to obtain	■ Placing greater reliance on judgment and experience ■ Improvising more; using data-intense approaches less (e.g., TQM) ■ Using outside expertise (e.g., consultants)
Clarity of solution	Problem very complex and breaking new ground; little existing data (but available)	■ Providing strong skills in data gathering, data analysis, and hypothesis testing ■ Tolerating ambiguity and taking time to roll around in the problem ■ Taking a flexible approach (or multiple approaches)

With these factors in mind, you can make an informed assessment of whether a given approach is appropriate for your current change challenge. In recent years many different performance-improvement processes have been developed and used with success in some situations. The good news is that their development has given RCLs an ever growing menu of approaches to consider. The bad news is that change leaders can err either by trying the latest fad in the wrong situation or by using the same approach in every situation.

Only by considering the strengths, weaknesses, and appropriate conditions of each process, relative to your current change situation, can you make an effective choice. As an example, here is a brief assessment of five common performance-improvement processes keyed to many of the factors cited above. You should make a similar assessment of any approaches you are considering.

STRUCTURED PERFORMANCE-IMPROVEMENT PROCESS	APPROPRIATE CONDITIONS (↑) AND STRENGTHS (+)	INAPPROPRIATE CONDITIONS (↓) AND POTENTIAL PITFALLS (−)
Quality programs (e.g., TQM)[3] Use of rigorous measurement and root cause analysis tools to systematically solve problems and incrementally improve performance	↑ Time available for learning ↑ Readily measurable processes and outputs + Skill and knowledge building + Continuous improvement	↓ Amorphous problems ↓ Rapidly changing environments − Becoming enamored of the concept vs. the objective − Activity vs. performance focus
Breakthrough teams[4] Small, cross-functional teams attack well-defined problems for which significant improvement is possible in 6–8 weeks	↑ Well-defined problems ↑ Good data availability + Sharp goal definition + Early wins to build confidence and momentum + Readily replicable (many teams on many problems)	↓ Large, complex problems ↓ Long lead or cycle times − Sustaining beyond initial gains
Reengineering[5] Redefinition and redesign of work flows from customer point of view to improve cost, quality, and speed	↑ Cross-functional problems and opportunities ↑ Information-intensive action flows + Reorientation from internal to external view + Reducing time and cost, and improving quality, of complex activities	↓ Strategy (customer needs and offering) unclear − Tweaking and paring vs. fundmental rethinking and redesigning − Focus only on headcount and cost reduction

[3] See David A. Garvin, *Managing Quality,* or Armand V. Feigenbaum, *Total Quality Control.*
[4] See Robert H. Schaffer, *The Breakthrough Strategy.*
[5] See James Champy and Michael Hammer, *Reengineering the Corporation.*

STRUCTURED PERFORMANCE-IMPROVEMENT PROCESS	APPROPRIATE CONDITIONS (↑) AND STRENGTHS (+)	INAPPROPRIATE CONDITIONS (↓) AND POTENTIAL PITFALLS (−)
Workout (GE model)[6] Front-line workers raise issues of low-value work and bottlenecks which management is obligated to address in real time	↑ Middle management blocking change from the bottom ↑ Early communications and awareness building + Action focused + Invigorating to work force	↓ Insufficient top leadership will to prod reluctant middle management ↓ High urgency; limited time
Workplace redesign[7] Teams redesign organization and work processes to improve performance and enhance job satisfaction	↑ Sufficient time available ↑ Employment (not job) security high ↑ Willing, skilled workforce + Skill and commitment building + Continuous improvement	↓ Broad, complex issues ↓ No clearly defined, natural work groups − Alignment with broader strategy − Internal vs. marketplace focus

[6] See Noel Tichy, *Control Your Destiny or Someone Else Will.*
[7] See Jack D. Orsburn et al., *Self-Directed Work Teams.*

Edging Out

If you have had a recent success with a performance improvement initiative, think about how you might build on it.

New horizons	List three ways to extend your intiative, e.g.: ■ Wider scale? Are there similar departments/locations where you might roll-out the approach (e.g., branch offices or other plants?)	1. _____ _____ _____
	■ Wider scope? Is it time to involve other functions to address the bigger issues (e.g., end-to-end process redesign)?	2. _____ _____ _____
	■ Tougher problems? Initial efforts often succeed by capturing the low-hanging fruit. Are there harder to reach opportunities that you now have the skills and experience to tackle?	3. _____ _____ _____
Expanded leadership	Think about developing the new leadership capacity required ■ Are there individuals involved in recent efforts who are ready to play larger roles? ■ Who are the new people who are critical to involve? ■ Do they have the required conviction, capability, and courage? ■ How can you make the opportunity clear and show people the pathway to improvement?	_____ _____ _____ _____ _____
Required adaptation	Consider how these new opportunities differ from the one you just tackled. ■ What factors are different? (e.g., wider scale or scope, tougher problem) ■ How must you modify your tools and approach? ■ What new tools are needed?	_____ _____ _____ _____

BALANCING THE MIX OF INITIATIVES

While individual change initiatives may involve just one area or dimension of an organization, an overall change program must include and balance initiatives across three dimensions: top-down, bottom-up, and cross-functional. Such overall design may seem beyond your domain, but your thinking and insight on adding new initiatives or rebalancing efforts can be very helpful to top management in shaping the overall program.

Start gathering your thoughts by mapping all the current initiatives you know of against the three dimensions. Then put down your ideas about what should be added, redirected, or halted. Next, start sharing your mapping and thoughts with fellow change leaders, refining the picture based on your discussions. You may find your initial effort leads to a needed overall assessment and redirection of the change program.

Top-down direction setting   *Current*   *Needed*

- Provide focus, overall vision   _____   _____
- Set goals   _____   _____
- Design overall program   _____   _____
- Clear roadblocks   _____   *Halt*
- Provide resources   _____   _____
- Communicate agenda; promote tools

Cross-functional process design   *Current*   *Needed*

- Address the business and management   _____   _____
  process flaws which block significant   _____   _____
  performance improvement   _____   _____
- Link activities and information together in _____   *Halt*
  new ways for performance breakthroughs   _____   _____

Bottom-up performance improvement   *Current*   *Needed*

- Unit by unit, team oriented   _____   _____
  - Problem solving   _____   _____
  - Work redesign   _____   _____
  - Skill building   _____   *Halt*
  - Goal setting and achievement   _____   _____

C. A PICTURE TO REMEMBER

BUILDING MOMENTUM

Momentum	=	Mass	×	Velocity

Number of committed people working to improve results

Speed at which results are realized and new initiatives ramp-up

- Start the geometry (focus on two, who can focus on four, etc.)
- Create opportunities to participate in change initiatives
- Trade-up at every opportunity
  - Rotate leadership positions
  - Refocus formal promotion criteria on change skills and experience
  - Refocus hiring criteria

Speed learning
- Add more, better, and better-matched tools
- Find best practices (internally and externally)
- Share best practices
- Compress cycle times on succeeding initiatives
- Create a common language of change

Reduce drag
- Develop working visions
- Keep the big picture in front of people
- Keep focus consistent
- Align management processes

As an RCL, you are working both to improve your organization's performance and increase its capacity and momentum for further performance improvement. With apologies to Sir Isaac Newton, keep this formula in mind.